The Dream Behind the Dome:

Judge Roy Hofheinz

Lisa Klobuchar

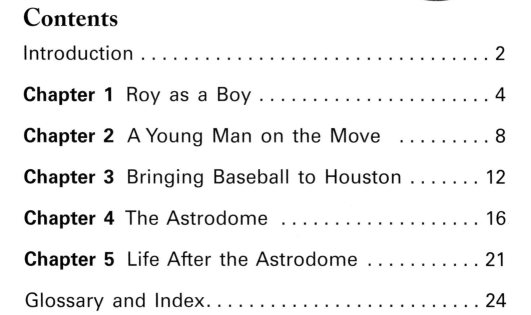

Contents

Rigby®

HOUGHTON MIFFLIN HARCOURT

www.Rigby.com
800-531-5015

Introduction

Would you pay to sit on hard seats and watch an outdoor baseball game when the temperature is over 100 degrees and bugs are biting you? Not many people would pay for that.

That was the problem facing officials in Houston, Texas, in the late 1950s. They wanted to bring major league baseball to their city, but it seemed as if it would always be a dream. But in Houston there was a man who knew how to make dreams come true. That dreammaker was Judge Roy Mark Hofheinz.

It could be very uncomfortable watching a baseball game, like this one, in Houston in the 1950s.

People liked listening to Roy talk about his ideas.

Even as a boy in Beaumont, Texas, Roy was special. He talked with so much energy that people knew he would do great things someday. Roy did grow up to do great things in Texas. He lived an interesting life and met many interesting people.

Chapter 1 Roy as a Boy

The Hofheinz family lived in a poor neighborhood in Beaumont, Texas. Roy's mother usually didn't allow her son to join in rough play with neighborhood children. Instead Roy spent many hours playing by himself around his family's house. He built his own "mud cities" with houses, roads, office buildings, and even bridges.

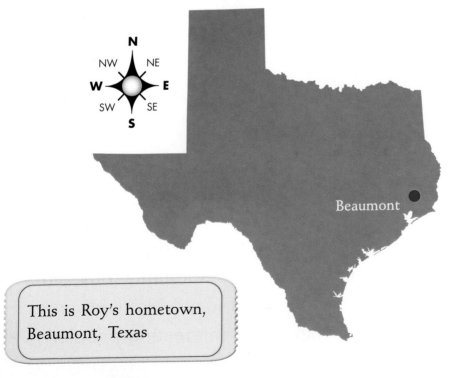

This is Roy's hometown, Beaumont, Texas

An Honest Worker

Roy was a good student and a dependable, honest worker. When he was 9 years old, he got a job at a local grocery store. One day the owner of the store told him to put only 14 ounces of beans in bags that were marked 16 ounces. Roy told his boss that he wouldn't do it because it was dishonest. Roy knew his boss was cheating customers. For example, if a 16-ounce bag of beans cost 32 cents, Roy knew that 1 ounce cost 2 cents. He also knew that 2 ounces were missing from each bag. Then he could figure out how much money his boss was taking from customers for each bag.

$$32 \div 16 = 2¢$$
$$16 - 14 = 2 \text{ ounces}$$
$$2 \times 2 = 4¢$$

How many bags would Roy's boss have sold in order to take 400 cents, or $4.00, from his customers?

Solve this: $n \times 4 = 400¢$

Answer: $100 \times 4 = 400$ cents

5

Roy the Businessman

When Roy was 12 years old, his father moved the family to Houston to find a better job. In high school, Roy created the first printed programs for his school's home football games so that people could read about the team. All by himself, Roy got businesses to pay for advertising space in the programs. He wrote, printed, and sold the programs at the games, and the principal of his school told him that he could keep any money that he made!

Roy earned money by selling programs at his school's home football games.

Roy used his car to advertise his dances.

When he was a little older, Roy also began to organize dances in Houston. People began hearing about the dances that were organized by Roy. He would rent the dance hall, book the bands, and advertise so people would come to his dances. (He would cover his car with dance posters and drive around town for everyone to see!)

Chapter 2   A Young Man on the Move

Roy graduated from high school when he was 16. He went to college and then to law school. By the time he was 19, Roy had already passed the bar exam, which was the test that made it possible for him to be a lawyer. But Roy was more interested in politics.

Roy studied to become a lawyer.

Judge R. Hofheinz

Roy's Political Life

In 1933 Roy married a woman named Irene, and they had three children—Roy, Jr., Fred, and Dene. In 1936 Roy was elected to the Texas House of Representatives. The voters elected him judge of Harris County in Houston two years later. Roy was a judge until 1946 when he was not elected again. But he used the title "Judge" for the rest of his life.

After being a judge, Roy decided to become a businessman, but he missed serving the people of Houston. He ran for mayor of Houston in 1952 and won. He was mayor for only two terms.

Changes in Houston

Roy made many improvements in Houston. He led the effort to build two **vehicle** tunnels and also had a modern highway system built.

The Baytown Tunnel is one of the vehicle tunnels that Judge Hofheinz had built in Houston.

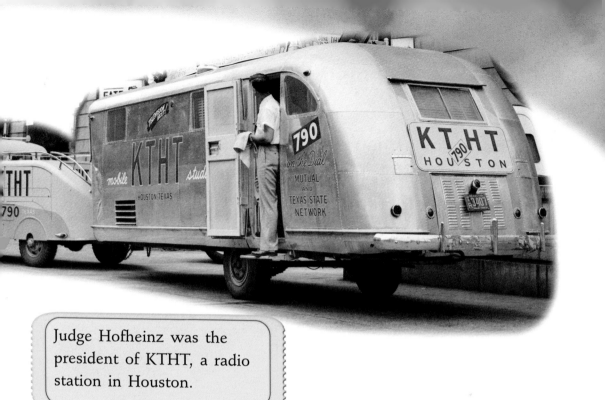

Judge Hofheinz was the president of KTHT, a radio station in Houston.

During the next few years, Judge Hofheinz bought and sold land, owned radio stations, and made plans to build an indoor, air-conditioned shopping mall. At the same time, some businessmen were trying to bring a major league baseball team to Houston. The problem was that major league team owners wouldn't let Houston have a team because the city didn't have a **stadium** for the games. And the city of Houston wouldn't build a stadium because it didn't have a team. It seemed hopeless.

Chapter 3 Bringing Baseball to Houston

The businessmen decided to ask Judge Hofheinz for help. Immediately the judge agreed that a baseball team and stadium for Houston were needed. But he strongly believed that people would not want to watch outdoor baseball in Houston. He knew that with the heat and rain in Houston, the best chance for success would be a covered stadium.

Planning for a Stadium

Hofheinz read every book he could find about the business of baseball and quickly became an expert. He helped think of a plan for an air-conditioned, domed stadium, and had a model built to show what it would look like. In October 1960, Hofheinz took his model of the stadium to the major league baseball owners' meeting in Chicago, Illinois. That afternoon Houston got its baseball team!

Building the Stadium

After over a year of planning, building the domed stadium began in January 1962. The Judge helped buy land and get money to pay for the stadium. He thought of most of the ideas for the stadium's features. He also worked with the builders to solve the many problems involved in building this stadium, such as where the people would park their cars.

Judge Hofheinz watched as the Astrodome was being built.

These astronauts threw out the first balls during an opening ceremony at the Astrodome.

Chapter 4 The Astrodome

The stadium was originally called the Harris County Stadium. But Hofheinz and his business partners announced that the domed stadium would be named the Astrodome and that the team name would be the Astros. (These names were used to honor the astronauts in the NASA space program that was in Houston.) In April 1965, over 42,000 fans cheered for the Astros as they played their first game in the Astrodome. One of those fans was Judge Roy's good friend, President Lyndon B. Johnson.

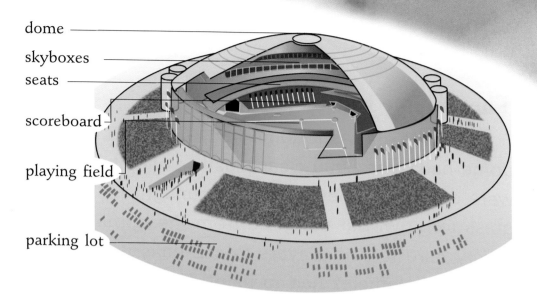

dome
skyboxes
seats
scoreboard
playing field
parking lot

A Special Place

Judge Hofheinz planned for the Astrodome to be outstanding, and it was. Fans sat in comfortable chairs, and there were several restaurants to choose from. The 4-story scoreboard was 474 feet long, and there were dazzling lights and sounds when the Astros scored or won a game. Judge Hofheinz created the idea of skyboxes, and these private seating areas were near the top of the dome. The stadium also had 53 places for wheelchairs and 30 areas where blind people could listen to the game on special radios.

The Trouble with Turf

Originally, the Astrodome had real grass. The dome had over 4,000 clear plastic skylights that were designed to let in enough sunlight for the grass to grow. But the glare from the dome made it very hard for the players to see balls flying in the air, so Hofheinz had to paint over the clear glass. Without sunlight the grass began to die.

The grass in the Astrodome began to die as soon as the skylights were painted.

Hofheinz thought that real grass would not grow in the Astrodome, and he had been talking with people who were developing a new kind of fake grass. These people told Judge Hofheinz that it would be four years before they completed the tests on the fake grass, but the judge needed it in less than a year!

Scientists needed time to develop a new kind of fake grass.

Hofheinz asked the company to send him large pieces of the fake grass, or **turf,** so that he could put it down in the Astrodome. Then he had football players, horses, and elephants walk all over it! He even drove a car on it!

The fake turf passed the tests, and the entire field was carpeted in time for the first 1966 preseason game. Naturally, the new fake turf was called AstroTurf®, after the Astros.

Comparing Grass and AstroTurf®

	Grass	AstroTurf®
Where do you find it?	It is outside.	It is inside.
How do you take care of it?	It needs to be cut and chemically treated.	It doesn't need to be cut or chemically treated.
Is it expensive to care for?	It's expensive to care for.	It is expensive to set up but costs nothing to care for.
How would you describe it?	It is green, alive, and can grow.	It is green, fake, and cannot grow.

Chapter 5 Life After the Astrodome

In 1965 Judge Hofheinz bought 147 **acres** of land around the Astrodome. In 1968 he opened a 57-acre amusement park there and called it AstroWorld™. The park had about 100 rides and outdoor air-conditioning for the comfort of the guests. Cool air blew on the waiting areas for rides, under picnic umbrellas, and on all other shaded areas!

> If Judge Hofheinz used 57 of his 147 acres for AstroWorld™, how many acres did he use for other projects?

Answer:
57 acres + n acres = 147 acres
57 acres + 90 acres = 147 acres

> AstroWorld™ was Judge Hofheinz's air-conditioned amusement park.

One More Business Deal

Judge Hofheinz had always loved the circus. When he heard that one of his friends was trying to buy a famous circus, he called his friend and asked to be his partner in the deal. In 1967 after more than a year of secret talks, Judge Hofheinz and his friend flew to Italy and signed the papers to become owners of the circus.

Judge Hofheinz loved the circus.

In 1970 Judge Hofheinz had a stroke and could no longer walk. He also owed a lot of money because of the many loans he had taken out to pay for his properties. It became difficult for him to repay the loans, and one by one, he had to give up his businesses.

Farewell to the Judge

Judge Roy Mark Hofheinz died in 1982. Before heading to the cemetery, the cars going to his funeral rode around the Astrodome twice. Without the judge's tireless work, good sales abilities, and creativity, that world-famous stadium never would have been built. It was a nice goodbye to the man who will always be remembered as the "Father of Indoor Baseball."

Glossary

acres   units of area used to measure land

stadium   a field for playing sports that is surrounded by many rows of seats

turf   fake or real grass

vehicle   a car, truck, or other object with wheels used to move around

Index